Measurei

Rashmi Gupta

Measurement of Software Quality Factors using CK Metrics

LAP LAMBERT Academic Publishing

Impressum / Imprint
Bibliografische Information der Deutschen Nationalbibliothek: Die Deutsche Nationalbibliothek verzeichnet diese Publikation in der Deutschen Nationalbibliografie; detaillierte bibliografische Daten sind im Internet über http://dnb.d-nb.de abrufbar.

Bibliographic information published by the Deutsche Nationalbibliothek: The Deutsche Nationalbibliothek lists this publication in the Deutsche Nationalbibliografie; detailed bibliographic data are available in the Internet at http://dnb.d-nb.de.

Coverbild / Cover image: www.ingimage.com

Verlag / Publisher:
LAP LAMBERT Academic Publishing
ist ein Imprint der / is a trademark of
OmniScriptum GmbH & Co. KG
Bahnhofstraße 28, 66111 Saarbrücken, Deutschland / Germany
Email: info@omniscriptum.com

Herstellung: siehe letzte Seite /
Printed at: see last page
ISBN: 978-3-659-89331-5

Zugl. / Approved by: Kurukshetra, Kurukshetra university, 2011

Contents

1. INTRODUCTION

1.1 OBJECTIVE OF THE THESIS WORK

Software engineering is a profession dedicated to analysis, designing, implementing and modifying software so that it is of high quality and fast to build. Software quality is the attribute to measure the software characteristics. To measure software quality, a no. of software metrics are used. Metric are the quantitative measure of the degree to which a system, component, or process possesses a given attribute.

Software metrics are quantifiable measures that can be used to measure different characteristics of a software system or software development process.

Measurement is the process by which numbers and symbols are assigned to attributes of entities in the real world in such a way as to describe them according to clear defined rules.

Object oriented metrics include three "traditional" metrics adapted for an object oriented environment, and six "new" metrics to evaluate the principle object oriented structures and concepts. The metrics focus on internal object structures that reflect the complexity of each individual entity, such as methods and classes, and on external complexity that measures the interactions among entities, such as coupling and inheritance. The metrics measure computational complexity that affects the efficiency of an algorithm and the use of machine resources, as well as psychological complexity factors that affect the ability of a programmer to create, comprehend, modify and maintain software.

But as important as the metrics chosen is what the metrics "tell" the developers and managers about the quality and object oriented structure of the design and code; metrics without interpretation guidelines are of little value. Metrics for object oriented development is a relatively new field of study, however, and have not reached maturity. Although some numeric thresholds are suggested by analysis developers, there is little application data to justify specific "good" and "bad" ranges. Traditional software metrics are used as object oriented metrics that support the goal of measuring design and code quality. The metrics evaluate the object oriented concepts: ***methods, classes, coupling,*** and ***inheritance***.

We support the use of three traditional metrics and present six additional metrics specifically for object oriented systems. Some researchers and practitioners contend traditional metrics are inappropriate for object oriented systems. There are valid reasons for applying traditional metrics, however, if it can be done. The traditional metrics have been widely used, they are well understood by researchers and practitioners, and their relationships to software quality attributes have been validated.

Software quality is measured in terms of software quality factors which affect it.

They can be broadly divided into two categories. The classification is done on the basis of measurability. The first category of the factors is of those that can be measured directly such as number of logical errors and the second category clubs those factors which can be measured only indirectly for example maintainability but the each of the factors are to be measured to check for the content and the quality control. Few factors of quality are available and they are mentioned below.

- **Correctness** - extent to which a program satisfies its specification and fulfills the client's objective.
- **Reliability** - extent to which a program is supposed to perform its function with the required precision.
- **Efficiency** - amount of computing and code required by a program to perform its function.
- **Integrity** - extent to which access to software and data is denied to unauthorized users.
- **Usability**- labor required to understand, operate, prepare input and interpret output of a program
- **Maintainability**- effort required to locate and fix an error in a program.
- **Flexibility**- effort needed to modify an operational program.
- **Testability**- effort required to test the programs for their functionality.
- **Portability**- effort required to run the program from one platform to other or to different hardware.
- **Reusability**- extent to which the program or it's parts can be used as building blocks or as prototypes for other programs.
- **Interoperability**- effort required to couple one system to another.

Now as you consider the above-mentioned factors it becomes very obvious that the measurements of all of them to some discrete value are quite an impossible task. Therefore, another method was evolved to measure out the quality. A set of matrices is defined and is used to develop expressions for each of the factors as per the following expression

Fq = C1*M1 + C2*M2 + ...Cn*Mn

where Fq is the software quality factor, Cn are regression coefficients and Mn is metrics that influences the quality factor.

Functionality is measured via the evaluation of the feature set and the program capabilities, the generality of the functions that are derived and the overall security of the system.

1.2 CONTRIBUTION AND ORGANIZATION OF THESIS

Main contributions of this thesis are:

- Software quality assessment.
- Study of CK metrics.
- Selection of the tools to evaluate ck metrics.
- Evaluation of software quality factor.

The thesis report is organized into six chapters. The chapter wise detail is given below:

Chapter 1: In this chapter, the objective of the thesis work is presented .The Design Methodology and Metrics Tools used.

Chapter 2: This chapter presents software quality and its quality factors.

Chapter 3: In this chapter, introduction to ck metrics is given.

Chapter 4: In this chapter, Literature Review is presented.

Chapter 5: In this chapter, brief introduction to the Eclipse Metric and ckjm tools are presented and ck metrics are generated.

Chapter 6: This chapter presents the equation for different software quality factors.

Chapter 7: This chapter presents the conclusion of the work done and future scope.

2. SOFTARE QUALITY

The American Heritage Dictionary defines quality as a "characteristic or attribute of something".

As an attribute of an item, quality refers to measurable characteristics- things we can measure to known standards such as length, color, electrical properties, and malleability. However, software, largely an intellectual entity, is more challenging to characterize than physical objects.

When we examine an item based on its measurable characteristics, two kinds of quality may be encountered: ***quality of design*** and ***quality of conformance***.

Quality of Design **refers to the characteristics that designers specify for an item.**

Quality of Conformance **is the degree to which the design specifications are followed during manufacturing [18].**

But according to Robert Glass, users' satisfaction is most important [18].

According to International Standards Organization quality is defined as: **"The totality of features and characteristics of a product or service that bear on its ability to satisfy specified or implied needs".**

According to IEEE Standard (IEEE Std 729-1983) definition of software quality:

"The totality of features and characteristics of a software product that bear on its ability to satisfy given needs: for example, conform to specifications.

The degree to which software possesses a desired combination of attributes.
The degree to which a customer or user perceives that software meets his or her composite expectations.
The composite characteristics of software that determine the degree to which the software in use will meet the expectations of the customer".

R.S.Pressman has emphasized on three important points:

1. Software requirements are the foundation from which quality is measured. Lack of conformance to requirements is lack of quality.
2. Specified standards define a set of development criteria that guide the manner in which software is engineered. If the criteria are not followed, lack of quality will almost surely result.

There is a set of implicit requirements that often goes unmentioned (e.g. the desire for ease of use). If software conforms to its explicit requirements but fails to meet implicit requirements, software quality is suspect.

2.2 Software Quality Model:

According to Wallmüller "one of the oldest and most frequently applied [software quality] models is that of McCall's Quality Model.

McCall propose a useful categorization of factors that affect software quality. These software quality factors focus on three important aspects of a software product:

- Its operational characteristics
- Its ability to undergo change
- Its adaptability to new environments.

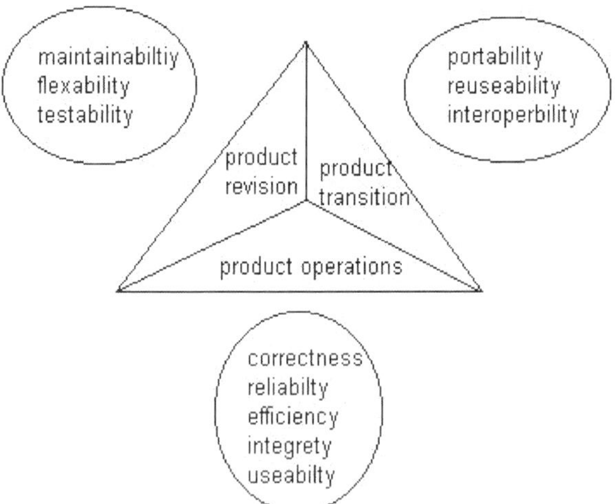

Fig 2.1: McCall's Software Quality Model

Referring to factors McCall provide following descriptions:

- Correctness: The extent to which a program satisfies its specifications and fulfills the customer's mission objectives.
- Reliability: The extent to which a program can be expected to perform its intended function with required precision.
- Efficiency: The amount of computing resources and code required by a program to perform its function.
- Integrity: The extent to which access to software or data by unauthorized persons can be controlled.
- Usability: The effort required to learn, operate, prepare input for and interpret output of a program.
- Maintainability: The effort required to locate and fix an error in a program.
- Flexibility: The effort required to modify an operational program.
- Testability: The effort required to test a program to ensure that it performs its intended function.
- Portability: The effort required to transfer the program from one hardware and/or software system environment to another.
- Reusability: The extent to which a program [or parts of program] can be reused in other applications – related to the packaging and scope of the functions that the program performs.
- Interoperability: The effort required to couple one system to another [5, 18].

2.2.1 Limitation of McCall's Quality Model

McCall include all dimensions and divide the quality attributes into these dimensions.

The limitation of McCall's Quality Model is that do not suggest any method to measure the quality factors either in structured programming or object oriented programming. We have removed this limitation by measuring the quality attributes of McCall's quality model.

2.2.2 Measurement of Quality Attributes

Quality attributes are affected by the values of CK metrics. This phenomenon helps us to measure the quality attributes. Based upon this phenomenon we can derive equations between quality attributes and CK metrics. Quality attributes can then be measured with help of these equations. This is the idea of our research work.

2.3 More on Quality Attributes

Following are the quality attributes of our proposed quality model:

2.3.1Usability

The effort required to learn, operate, prepare input for and interpret output of a program.

To illustrate this point, some broad definitions of usability from three different standards are listed next:

"A set of attributes that bear on the effort needed for use and on the individual assessment

of such use, by a stated or implied set of users" (ISO/IEC 9126, 1991).

"The extent to which a product can be used by specified users to achieve specified goals

with effectiveness, efficiency and satisfaction in a specified context of use" (ISO 9241−11,

1998).

"The ease with which a user can learn to operate, prepare inputs for, and interpret outputs

of a system or component" (IEEE Std.610.12-1990).

2.3.2 Maintainability

Every software program needs to be changed to meet the changing requirements of users and customers during its lifetime. It is generally impractical and uneconomical to produce software, which does not need to be changed. Introduction of new hardware also necessitates the change in the software. The process of changing software after it has been delivered and is in use is called software maintenance [26]. This is a task that every development group has to face when the software is delivered to the customer's site, installed and is operational. Some software may be maintained for several decades. Initially, aim of the software development was to write working programs. Then the aim shifts to write good quality programs, but lastly the aim is to write good maintainable programs. It has been reported that amount of effort spent on maintenance is between 65% and 75% of total software development and support efforts [25]. Despite the fact that software maintenance is very important and challenging task, it is poorly managed. One reason for poor management is the lack of a good measure of software maintainability. The fundamental reality that "you can not control what you can not measure" highlights the importance of a good measurement of software maintainability [28].

2.3.3 Testability

Software testability is affected by many different factors, including the required validity, the process and tools used and the representation of the requirements. Voas et. al. [27] defines software testability as the probability that a piece of software will fail on its next execution during testing, provided it contains a fault. This *fault sensitivity* is obtained by multiplying the probabilities that

1. The location containing the fault is executed;

2. The fault corrupts the program's state;

3. The corrupted state gets propagated to the output.

High fault sensitivity indicates high testability and vice versa.

2.3.4 Reliability

IEEE 610.12-1990 defines reliability as "The ability of a system or component to perform its required functions under stated conditions for a specified period of time." IEEE 982.1-1988 defines Software Reliability Management as "The process of optimizing the reliability of software through a program that emphasizes software error prevention, fault detection and removal, and the use of measurements to maximize reliability in light of project constraints such as resources, schedule and performance." Using these definitions, software reliability is comprised of three activities:

1. Error prevention

2. Fault detection and removal

3. Measurements to maximize reliability, specifically measures that support the first two activities

There has been extensive work in measuring reliability using mean time between failure and mean time to failure [30]. Successful modeling has been done to predict error rates and reliability. These activities address the first and third aspects of reliability, identifying and removing faults so that the software works as expected with the specified reliability. In our research work we have predicted reliability for OO software. We have predicted reliability from fault proneness of a class using CK metrics [33].

2.3.5 Flexibility

The ease with which a system or component can be modified for use in applications or environments other than those for which it was specifically designed. To measure software flThe ability of software to change easily in response to different user and system requirements.

Texibility in precise terms, we introduce the notion of evolution complexity and demonstrate how it can be used to measure and compare the flexibility of:

1. Programming paradigms

2. Architectural styles

3. Design patterns

3. Software Metrics

All engineering disciplines have metrics (such as metrics for weight are grams, pound; metrics for length are meters, inches; temperature has metrics Celsius, Kelvin) to quantify various characteristics of their process, products and measure. Since software has no physical attributes, conventional metrics are not helpful. A number of metrics have been proposed to quantify things like size, complexity of the software product. Metrics for size is LOC, complexity has McCabe's Cyclomatic Complexity and reliability has metrics like Mean Time to Failure (MTTF). [19]

The IEEE Standard Glossary defines metric as "a quantitative measure of the degree to which a system, component, or process possesses a given attribute."[18]

Software metrics are quantifiable measures that can be used to measure different characteristics of a software system or software development process.

Measurement is the process by which numbers and symbols are assigned to attributes of entities in the real world in such a way as to describe them according to clear defined rules [17]. Measurement can be of two types:

- **Direct Measurement:** Direct measurement of an attribute is measurement which does not depend on the measurement of any other attribute. e.g. size can be measured in LOC.
- **Indirect Measurement:** Indirect measurement of an attribute is measurement which involves the measurement of one or more attributes. Effort can be measured by measuring size.

Direct measures are generally easier to collect than indirect measures. Size-oriented metrics are used to collect direct measures of software engineering output and quality. Function-oriented metrics provide indirect measures [19].

Object oriented metrics include three "traditional" metrics adapted for an object oriented environment, and six "new" metrics to evaluate the principle object oriented structures and concepts. The metrics focus on internal object structures that reflect the complexity of each individual entity, such as methods and classes, and on external complexity that measures the interactions among entities, such as coupling and inheritance. The metrics measure computational complexity that affects the efficiency of an algorithm and the use of machine resources, as well as psychological complexity factors that affect the ability of a programmer to create, comprehend, modify and maintain software.

But as important as the metrics chosen is what the metrics "tell" the developers and managers about the quality and object oriented structure of the design and code; metrics without interpretation guidelines are of little value. Metrics for object oriented development is a relatively new field of study, however, and have not reached maturity. Although some numeric thresholds are suggested by analysis developers, there is little application data to justify specific "good" and "bad" ranges. Traditional software metrics are used as object oriented metrics that support the goal of measuring design and code quality. The metrics evaluate the object oriented concepts: ***methods, classes, coupling,*** and ***inheritance***.

We support the use of three traditional metrics and present six additional metrics specifically for object oriented systems. Some researchers and practitioners contend traditional metrics are inappropriate for object oriented systems. There are valid reasons for applying traditional metrics, however, if it can be done. The traditional metrics have been widely used, they are well understood by researchers and practitioners, and their relationships to software quality attributes have been validated. Table 1.1 presents an overview of the metrics for object oriented systems. The first three metrics in Table 1 are examples of traditional metrics applied to the object oriented structure of methods instead of functions or procedures. The next six metrics are specifically for object oriented systems and the object oriented construct applicable is indicated [3].

SOURCE	METRIC	OBJECT-ORIENTED CONSTRUCT
Traditional	Cyclomatic complexity (CC)	Method
	Lines of Code(LOC)	Method
	Comment Percentage (CP)	Method
CK Object Oriented Metric	Weighted Methods per Class (WMC)	Method
	Response for a Class (RFC)	Class/Method
	Lack of Cohesion of Methods (LCOM)	Class/Cohesion
	Coupling Between Objects (CBO)	Coupling
	Depth of Inheritance Tree (DIT)	Inheritance
	Number of Children (NOC)	Inheritance

Table 3.1: Metrics for Object Oriented Systems

3.1Traditional Metrics

There are many metrics that are applied to traditional functional development. It has been has identified three of these metrics that are applicable to object oriented development: Complexity, Size, and Readability. To measure the complexity, the cyclomatic complexity is used.

METRIC 1: Cyclomatic Complexity (CC)

Cyclomatic Complexity was first proposed as a measurement of a modules logical complexity by T.J McCabe in 1976. The primary purpose of the metric is to evaluate the test- and maintainability of software modules, and it has therefore been widely used in research areas concerned with maintenance. There is a strong correlation between the McCabe metric and the number of errors existing in source code, as well as the time required to find and correct such errors. It is more difficult to find it practically, but the measure can be a good indicator of the complexity of a method.

Since the CC metric is a measure of complexity it is desirable to keep it as low as possible. The upper limit of CC has been suggested10 as a practical upper limit.

Definition

McCabe's CC metric is defined as:

$v(G) = e - n + 2$

where $v(G)$ = the cyclomatic complexity of the flow graphG of the module,

e = the number of edges in G and n = the number of nodes in G.

To illustrate this definition consider this pseudo code example of a sorting algorithm:

```
bubbleSort(array A)

do while A not sorted set A as sorted

for i=1 until i<A.size do

if A.[i] < A.[i-1]

swap(A[i-1],A[i]) set A as unsorted

end_if
```

6: end_for

7: end_while

8: end_bubbleSort

Now all we have to do is convert this code segment into a flow graph in order to calculate the cyclomatic complexity. This is done by using the numbers that indicate the statements in the code above, as nodes in our flow graph:

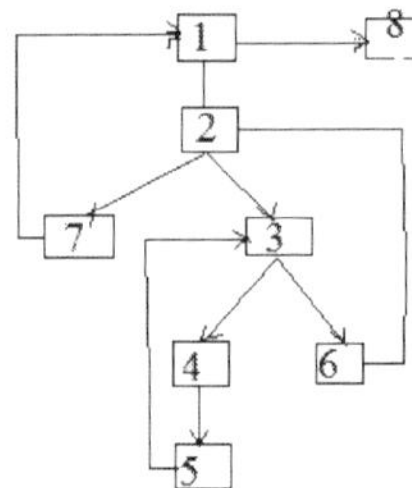

Figure 3.1: flow graph representation.

The number of edges = 10 and number of nodes = 8 this yields a CC value v(G) = 10 – 8 + 2 = 4.

One more way to calculate v(G) is:

v(G) = P+1

where P is the number of predicate nodes* found in G. In figure 2.1 nodes number 1,2 and 3 (the double squared nodes) are predicate nodes and thus gives a value of v(G) = 3+1 = 4.

* A predicate node is a node that represents a Boolean statement in the code, thus giving it two outgoing edges instead of one.

METRIC 2: Size

Size of a class is used to evaluate the ease of understanding of code by developers and maintainers. Size can be measured in a variety of ways. These include counting all physical lines of code, the number of statements, the number of blank lines, and the number of comment lines. Lines of Code (LOC) count all lines. Non-comment Non-blank (NCNB) is sometimes referred to as Source Lines of Code and counts all lines that are not comments and not blanks. Executable Statements (EXEC) is a count of executable statements regardless of number of physical lines of code. For example, in FORTRAN and *IF* statement may be written:

IF X = 3

Then

This example would be 3 LOC, 3 NCNB, and 1 EXEC.

Executable statements is the measure least influenced by programmer or language style. Thresholds for evaluating the meaning of size measures vary depending on the coding language used and the complexity of the method. However, since size affects ease of understanding by the developers and maintainers, classes and methods of large size will always pose a higher risk [3].

METRIC 3: Comment Percentage

The line counts done to compute the Size metric can be expanded to include a count of the number of comments, both on-line (with code) and stand-alone. The comment percentage is calculated by the total number of comments divided by the total lines of code less the number of blank lines. Since comments assist developers and maintainers, higher comment percentages increase understandability and maintainability [3].

3.2 Chidamber and Kemerer Metrics

Chidamber and Kemerer's metrics suite for object-oriented design is the deepest research in OO metrics investigation. They have defined six metrics for OO design.

METRIC 4: Weighted Methods per Class (WMC)

Chidamber and C.F Kemerer first proposed the WMC metric in 1991 and it relates directly to the definition of complexity of an object. The number of methods and the complexity of methods involved are indicators of how much time and effort is required to develop and maintain the object The larger the number of methods in an object, the greater the potential impact on the children, since, children will inherit all the methods in the object.

Since WMC can be described as an extension of the CC metric (if CC is used to calculate WMC) that applies to objects, its recommended threshold value can be compared with the upper limit of the CC metric. Take the calculated WMC value and divide it with the number of methods, this value can then be compared with the upper limit of CC. One disadvantage of using CC in order to measure an objects complexity is that the WMC value cannot be collected in early design stages, e.g. when the methods in a class has been defined but not implemented. To be able to measure WMC as early as possible one could use the number of methods in a class as a complexity value, but then the WMC metric is no longer a complexity measure but a size measure, also known as the number of methods metric.

Definition

Consider a class C_1, with methods M_1, M_2, …M_n. Let c_1, c_2, …c_n be the static complexity of the methods. Then:

WMC = $\Sigma_i^n c_i$, where n is the number of methods in the class.

If all static complexities are considered to be unity, WMC = n, the number of methods.

The static complexity of a method can be measured in many ways (e.g. cyclomatic complexity) and the developers of this metric leave this to be an implementation decision.

METRIC 5: Response for a Class (RFC)

The RFC is the count of the set of all methods that can be invoked in response to a message to an object of the class or by some method in the class. This includes all methods accessible within the class hierarchy. This metric looks at the combination of the complexity of a class through the number of methods and the amount of communication with other classes. The larger the number of methods that can be invoked from a class through messages, the greater the complexity of the class. If a large number of methods can be invoked in response to a message, the testing and debugging of the class becomes complicated since it requires a greater level of understanding on the part of the tester. A worst case value for possible responses will assist in the appropriate allocation of testing time [2, 3].

Definition

RFC = |RS| where RS is the response set for the class, given by

RS = $\{M\}\ U_{\text{all } i}\ \{R_i\}$

where $\{R_i\}$ = set of methods called by method i and

{M} = set of all methods in the class.

To illustrate this definition consider the following example:

A::f1() calls B::f2()

A::f2() calls C::f1()

A::f3() calls A::f4()

A::f4() calls no method

Then RS = {A::f1, A::f2, A::f3, A::f4} U {B::f2} U {C::f1} U {A::f4}

= {A::f1, A::f2, A::f3, A::f4, B::f2, C::f1}

and RFC = 6

METRIC 6 – Lack of Cohesion (LCOM)

The cohesion of a class is characterized by how closely the local methods are related to the local instance variables in a class.The LCOM metric is a value of the dissimilarity of the methods in a class. A high LCOM value in a class indicates that it might be a good idea to split the class into two or more sub-classes. Since the class might have too many different tasks to perform, it is better (design-wise) to use more specific objects. Because LCOM is a value of dissimilarity of methods, it helps to identify flaws in the design of classes. Cohesiveness of methods within a class is desirable, since it promotes encapsulation and decreases complexity of objects.

Chidamber-Kemerer Definition

Consider a class C_1 with n methods M_1, M_2, ..., M_n. Let $\{I_j\}$ = set of instance variables used by method M_i. There are n such sets $\{I_1\}$, ..., $\{I_n\}$. Let $P = \{(I_i, I_j) \mid I_i \cap I_j = ø\}$ and $Q = \{(I_i, I_j) \mid I_i \cap I_j \neq ø\}$. If all n sets $\{I_1\}$, ..., $\{I_n\}$ are ø then let P = ø.

LCOM = |P| - |Q|, if |P| > |Q| = 0 otherwise [7].

The definition of disjointness of sets given in the Chidamber-Kemerer definition is somewhat ambiguous, and was further defined by Li and Henry.

Li-Henry Definition

LCOM* = number of disjoint sets of local methods; no two sets intersect; any two methods in the same set share at least one local instance variable; ranging from 0 to N; where N is a positive integer.

To illustrate these two different definitions consider the following example:

Given a class C and its variables a, b, c and d the following methods are present:

Method W accesses variables {a, b}.

Method X accesses variable {c}.

Method Y accesses no variables.

Method Z accesses {b, d}.

Using the Li and Henry definition of the LCOM metric (LCOM*), the disjoint sets of methods, where any two methods in the same set share at least one local instance variable, would be:

$\{W, Z\}, \{X\}, \{Y\}$

The result is three different sets and thus the LCOM value is 3.

Using the definition proposed by Chidamber and Kemerer to calculate LCOM:

$W \cap X = ø$

$W \cap Y = ø$

$W \cap Z = \{b\}$

$X \cap Y = ø$

$X \cap Z = ø$

$Y \cap Z = ø$

P = 5, the intersections whose result is ø. Q = 1, the intersections whose result is not ø.

$LCOM = |P| - |Q| = 5 - 1 = 4$.

Another example where these two definitions return different values is in the case of a perfectly cohesive class (all methods are related to one and other), where measured by the Li and Henry metric, LCOM would have a value of 1 (one set of methods), whereas the same class would have a value of 0 when measured with Chidamber and Kemerer's metric ($|Q| > |P|$). In the case of a perfect un-cohesive class the value of the Li and Henry metric would equal the number of methods in the class. The same class measured with the CK metric would yield a higher value since the metric would equal to n taken two at a time ($((\frac{1}{2} n)(n-1))$, $n>1$), where n is the number of methods in the class. Take for instance three classes: A, B and C containing 3, 4, respective 5 methods that doesn't intersect one and another, the CK metric will return the values: 3, 6 respective 10 (all methods taken two at a time), while LH's metric results in the values: 3, 4 respective 5 (the number of different sets of non-intersected methods).

METRIC 7: Coupling Between Object Classes (CBO)

Coupling between Object Classes (CBO) is a count of the number of other classes to which a class is coupled. Excessive coupling is detrimental to modular design and prevents reuse. The more independent a class is, the easier it is reuse in another application. The larger the number of couples, the higher the sensitivity to changes in other parts of the design and therefore maintenance is more difficult. Strong coupling complicates a system since a class is harder to understand, change or correct by itself if it is interrelated with other classes. Complexity can be reduced by designing systems with the weakest possible coupling between classes. This improves modularity and promotes encapsulation [2, 3].

METRIC 8: Depth of Inheritance Tree (DIT)

Inheritance is when a class share the same structure or behaviour defined in another class. When a subclass inherits from one superclass it's called a single inheritance and when a subclass inherits from more than one superclass it's called multiple inheritance. Inheritance through classes increases its efficiency by reducing the redundancy. But the deeper the inheritance hierarchy is, the greater the probability is that it gets complicated and hard to predict its behaviour.

The depth of a class within the inheritance hierarchy is the maximum number of steps from the class node to the root of the tree and is measured by the number of ancestor classes. The deeper a class is within the hierarchy, the greater the number methods it is likely to inherit making it more complex to predict its behavior. Deeper trees constitute greater design complexity, since more methods and classes are involved, but the greater the potential for reuse of inherited methods. A support metric for DIT is the number of methods inherited (NMI).

Chidamber-Kemerer Definition

Depth of inheritance of the class is the DIT metric for the class. In cases involving multiple inheritances, the DIT will be the maximum length from the node to the root of the tree.

METRIC 9: Number of Children (NOC)

The number of children is the number of immediate subclasses subordinate to a class in the hierarchy. It is an indicator of the potential influence a class can have on the design and on the system. The greater the number of children, the greater the likelihood of improper abstraction of the parent and may be a case of misuse of sub classing. But the greater the number of children, the greater the reuse since inheritance is a form of reuse. If a class has a large number of children, it may require more testing of the methods of that class, thus increase the testing time [2, 3].

Definition

NOC = number of immediate subclasses subordinated to a class in the class hierarchy [7].

According to the definition of NOC only the immediate subclasses are counted, but a class has influence over all its subclasses.

4. LITERATURE SURVEY

It has been widely recognized that an important component of process improvement is the ability to measure the process. Given the central role that software development plays in the delivery and application of information technology, managers are increasingly focusing on process improvement in the software development area. This emphasis has had two effects. The first is that this demand has spurred the provision of a number of new and/or improved approaches to software development, with perhaps the most prominent being object orientation (00). Second, the focus on process improvement has increased the demand for software measures, or metrics with which to manage the process. The need for such metrics is particularly acute when an organization is adopting a new technology for which established practices have yet to be developed. Chidamber and Kemerer address these needs through the development and implementation of a new suite of metrics for 00 designs. Previous research on software metrics, while contributing to the field's understanding of software development processes, have generally been subject to one or more types of criticisms. These include: lacking a theoretical basis [6, 7] lacking in desirable measurement properties [8], being insufficiently generalized or too implementation technology dependent, and being too labor-intensive to collect [9].

Chidamber and Kemerer have proposed six design metrics, and analytically evaluated against a previously proposed set of measurement principles. An automated data collection tool was then developed and implemented to collect an empirical sample of these metrics at two field sites in order to demonstrate their feasibility and to suggest ways in which managers may use these metrics for process improvement.

These metrics are based in measurement theory and also reflect the viewpoints of experienced 00 software developers. In evaluating these metrics against a set of standard criteria, they are found to both

a) possess a number of desirable properties, and

b) suggest some ways in which the 00 approach may differ in terms of desirable or necessary design features from more traditional approaches [2].

Since object oriented technology uses objects and not algorithms as its fundamental building blocks, the approach to software metrics for object oriented programs must be different from the standard metrics set. Some metrics, such as lines of code and cyclomatic complexity, have become accepted as "standard" for traditional functional/ procedural programs, but for object oriented, there are many proposed object oriented metrics in the literature. The question is, "Which object oriented metrics should a project use, and can any of the traditional metrics be adapted to the object oriented environment?"

The Software Assurance Technology Center (SATC) at NASA Goddard Space Flight Center discusses its approach to choosing metrics for a project by first identifying the attributes associated with object oriented development. Within this framework, nine metrics for object oriented are selected. These metrics include three traditional metrics adapted for an object oriented environment, and six CK metrics to evaluate the principle object oriented structures and concepts. The metrics are first defined, then using a very simplistic object oriented example, the metrics are applied. Interpretation guidelines are then discussed and data from NASA projects are used to demonstrate the application of the metrics.

The SATC has found that a combination of traditional metrics and metrics that measure structures unique to object oriented development is most effective. This allows developers to continue to apply metrics that they are familiar with, such as complexity and lines of code to a new development environment. However, now that new concepts and structures are being applied, such inheritance, coupling, cohesion, methods and classes, metrics are needed to evaluate the effectiveness of their application. Metrics such as Weighted Methods per Class, Response for a Class, and Lack of Cohesion are applied to these areas. The application of a hierarchical structure also needs to be evaluated through metrics such as Depth in Tree and Number of Children [3].

R. Harrison, S. J. Counsell, R. V. Nithi considers empirical evidence in support of a set of object-oriented design metrics of Chidamber and Kemerer, and their applicability in different application domains. They briefly describe the metrics, and present empirical findings, arising from analysis of systems taken from a number of different application domains. The investigation has led to conclude that a subset of the metrics can be of great value to software developers, maintainers and project managers. They suggested that the set of metrics proposed by Chidamber and Kemerer represents a minimal set which addresses many of the main concerns of OO designers: coupling, cohesion, inheritance and class size, and was among the first to address such fundamental OO design issues [14]. Previously, metrics focusing on OO design had remained largely neglected. Evidence of the utility of the C&K metrics has been supported empirically in two OO industrial sites, adding credibility to the claims for the utility of metrics [2]. Since their inception, a number of criticisms have been made of the C&K metrics in terms of their validity and practicality [10, 11, 12, and 13]. However, the C&K metrics have been instrumental in promoting a debate in the metrics community about what constitutes a valid metric, and also spawned a large body of work in the areas of empirical software engineering. Finally, the C&K metrics have permitted researchers to learn more about OO systems, particularly about the features of OO systems which need to be urgently addressed. These results show that the C&K metrics can be used by developers and maintainers to gain insights into their systems' architectures. With large, complicated systems this information could prove to be very valuable to maintainers of legacy code as additional design documentation [14].

With object-oriented analysis and design methodologies gaining popularity, it is time to start investigating object-oriented metrics with respect to software quality. While metrics for the traditional functional decomposition and data analysis design approach measure the design structure and/or data structure independently, object-oriented metrics must be able to focus on the combination of function and data as an integrated object [2]. The evaluation of the utility of a metric as a quantitative measure of software quality was based on the measurement of a software quality attribute. The metrics selected, however, are useful in a wide range of models. Product Quality for code and design has five attributes. These are Efficiency, Complexity, Understandability, Reusability, and Testability/Maintainability. The SATC has proposed nine metrics for object-oriented systems. They cover the key concepts for object-oriented designs: methods, classes, cohesion, coupling, and inheritance [15, 16].

In a case study, Ping Yu Tarja Syst¨a empirically validated a set of object-oriented metrics in terms of their usefulness in predicting fault proneness, an important software quality indicator. In software forward engineering, software metrics are traditionally used to revise an improper design in an early phase of the software life cycle. Inadequacies and defects found can be modified and revised with considerably less costs and efforts than in later design phases or during software maintenance. Metrics data provides quick feedback to software engineers. By analyzing the collected data, complexity and design quality as well as some other properties of the final software can be predicted. This early feedback enables software designers and developers to correct the inadequacies in their design or implementation without too much effort. If appropriately used, it can lead to a significant reduction in costs of the overall implementation and improvements in quality of the final software product. The improved quality, in turn, reduces future maintenance efforts. The metrics data also helps project managers to make decisions on project priorities, personnel assignments, cost organization, and other resource allocations. However, information available in the early design phase is often inaccurate and insufficient. In fact, many useful metrics cannot be used during the early design phase. Because of this, information of software design presented by metric data needs to be revisited and acquired in various phases of the software life cycle. During the software testing phase, software metrics are particularly useful. With the metrics data, various software quality attributes can be unveiled to optimize resource allocation for testing. For instance, more time or personnel can be assigned to fault-prone modules that are identified with appropriately collected software metrics data. Since testing effort counts for approximately 30-50% of the total development effort [20], improving the efficiency of software testing will significantly shorten the software development cycle. Again, the more errors are found, the better the quality and maintainability of the software. Even though a great deal of research has investigated software metrics, important questions remain to be answered. Among them, a relevant question is what and how internal software metrics relate to external software attributes such as software quality, which is most useful but difficult to measure objectively. Ping Yu Tarja Syst¨a aimed at answering this question for object-oriented systems. He empirically validates a set of OO metrics in terms of their usefulness in predicting an important software quality indicator, *fault-proneness* [21].

Li and Henry conducted a case study with the goal to find OO metrics that correlated with maintainability. They have studied two commercial systems by validating the maintenance effort put in to them during three years. The systems they have studied are: UIMS™ (User Interface System) and QUES™ (Quality Evaluation System). Both systems where built using Classic-Ada™ which is an object oriented design/programming language developed by Software Productivity Solutions Inc. The maintenance effort is measured by the number of lines that have changed in a class during the three years they have collected the measurement. Their definition of a line change is: deletion of a line, addition of a line or a change in a line. This measurement they use in their case study to estimate the maintainability of the OO systems [22]. Software testability is affected by many different factors, including the required validity, the process and tools used, the representation of the requirements, and so on. Bruntink and Deursen investigate testability from the perspective of unit testing, where units consist of the classes of an object-oriented software system. They evaluated a set of object-oriented metrics with respect to their capabilities to predict the effort needed for testing [23].

Lionel C. Briand, John W. Daly empirically explored the relationships between existing object-oriented coupling, cohesion, and inheritance measures and the probability of fault detection in system classes during testing. In other words, the relationship between existing design measurement in OO systems and the quality of the software developed. They proposed an investigation and analysis strategy to make these kind of studies more repeatable and comparable. The results show that many of the measures capture similar dimensions in the data set, thus reflecting the fact that many of them are based on similar principles and hypotheses. However, it is shown that by using a subset of measures, accurate models can be built to predict which classes contain most of the existing faults. When predicting fault-prone classes, the best model shows a percentage of correct classifications higher than 80% and finds more than 90% of faulty classes. Besides the size of classes, the frequency of method invocations and the depth of inheritance hierarchies seem to be the main driving factors of fault proneness.

Kitchenham and Walker writes about the classical principles of dividing quality into a number of quality factors. The quality factors themselves are broken further down into lower level quality criteria.

The most widely accepted classification about software quality factors is by McCall, Richards

and Walters. They specify the relationship of different criteria to quality factors(/metrics). The factors listed by McCall and Arthur are as follows: correctness, reliability, efficiency, integrity, usability, maintainability, flexibility, testability, portability, reusability and interoperability. The underlying criteria for the factors are the attributes of the software product or software production process by which the factors can be judged or defined.

Different type of metrics exists. Examples of classical product oriented metrics are McCabe's cyclomatic complexity and lines of code (LOC).

Lines of code (LOC) metric are the best known metric among all software metrics. The LOC measure itself is not productivity metric, but combined with a measure of person/months will produce the needed metric.

Complexity metrics

A definition by Curtis follows: "Complexity is a characteristic of the software interface

which influences the resources another system will expand or commit while interacting with the

software.

The lines of code (LOC) metric has also been proposed as a complexity metric. The problems

with the LOC metric as a complexity measure is for instance that structured programs are

more readable and hence easier to maintain.

McCabe has proposed a complexity metric based on mathematical graph theory.

A program should be viewed as a graph with a single entry and a single exit point. Using

graph theory it is possible to state the number of basic paths through the control graph. The

complexity of a program is defined in terms of its control structure and is represented by the

maximum number of 'linearly independent' paths through the program. The formula for the

cyclomatic complexity number proposed by McCabe is then:

$v(G) = e - n + 2p$

where e = the number of edges in the graph

n = the number of nodes in the graph

p = the number of connected components in the graph

An "edge" in a flowgraph is a line connecting blocks of code that indicates flow of control. The blocks of code are considered "nodes". A procedure is considered a "connected component". The cyclomatic complexity for a multi-module program is the sum of the v's for the individual modules. The cyclomatic complexity number attempts to answer the question of how to build a modular system that are both easily maintainable and testable. McCabe writes that complexity less than or equal to 10 seems to provide reasonably modular programs. According to Arthur the cyclomatic complexity metric is based on the number of decision elements (IF-THEN-ELSE, DO WHILE, DO UNTIL, CASE) in the language and the number of AND, OR, and NOT phrases in each decision. The formula of the metric follows:

cyclomatic complexity = number of decisions + number of conditions + 1

The calculated counts represent "the total number of structural test paths in the program" and "the sum of the logic in the program".

Amandeep Kaur, Satwinder Singh analysed the CK metrics empirically. The CK metrics are evaluated empirically to much regarding the usefulness of the metrics to assess external attributes such as quality and maintainability. One of the suite of OO design measure was proposed by Chidamber and Kemerer. These metrics can aid users in understanding object oriented design complexity and in predicting external software qualities such as software defects, testing, and maintenance effort. Use of the CK set of metrics and other complexity measures are gradually growing in industry acceptance. This is reflected in the increasing number of industrial software tools, such as Rational Rose, that enable automated computation of these metrics. Even though this metric suite is widely, empirical validations of these metrics in real world software development setting are limited. Various flaws and inconsistencies have been observed in the suite of six class based metrics. They validated some solutions to some of these anomalies and clarified some important aspects of OO design, using Six projects in particular those aspects that may cause difficulties when attempting to define accurate and meaningful metrics.

CK Metrics by Abreu et al introduces that these attributes can express the quality of internal structure, thus being strongly correlated with quality characteristics like analyzability, changeability, stability and testability, which are important to software developers and maintainers.

Rosenberg, et al evaluated the Quality Assurance of Object Oriented Assurance and Risk Assessment of Object Oriented Metrics.

Briand, et al gives framework for cohesion and coupling measurement in Object Oriented System.

Linda, et al concluded that, as the fundamental building block of metric is object not algorithm, the approach to S/W metrics for Object Oriented Program.

Aggarwal et al proposed a set of metrics that are related to various constructs like class, coupling, cohesion, information hiding, polymorphism, reusability.

Cem Kaner, Senior Member, IEEE, and Walter P. Bond discussed about metrics:what do they measure? and how do we know? that we're measuring the attribute that we think we're measuring? These metrics are discussed in formal, theoretical ways in the computing literature (in terms of the representational theory of measurement) but rarely in simpler ways that foster application by practitioners. In the IEEE Standard 1061, direct measures need not be validated. "Direct" measurement of an attribute involves a metric that depends only on the value of the attribute, but few or no software engineering attributes or tasks are so simple that measures of them can be direct. Thus, all metrics should be validated. They continued with a framework for evaluating proposed metrics, and applied it to two uses of bug counts. Bug counts capture only a small part of the meaning of the attributes they are being used to measure. Multidimensional analyses of attributes appear promising as a means of capturing the quality of the attribute in question. Analysis fragments run throughout the paper, illustrating the breakdown of an attribute or task of interest into sub-attributes for grouped study.

Robert Austin provided an excellent discussion of the problems of measurement distortion and dysfunction in general. They explored one aspect of the problem of dysfunction. We assert that Software Engineering as a field presents an approach to measurement that underemphasizes

measurement validity (the condition that the measurement actually measures the attribute in question). This has a likely consequence: if a project or company is managed according to

the results of measurements, and those metrics are inadequately validated, insufficiently understood, and not tightly linked to the attributes they are intended to measure, measurement

distortions and dysfunctional should be commonplace.

They defined measurement presented by several authors and distinguished between them later.

"Measurement is the assignment of numbers to objects or events according to rule. [4] The rule of assignment can be any consistent rule. The only rule not allowed would be random assignment, for randomness amounts in effect to a nonrule."

"Measurement is the process of empirical, objective, assignment of numbers to properties of objects or events of the real world in such a way as to describe them."

"Measurement is the process by which numbers or symbols are assigned to attributes of entities in the real world in such a way as to characterize them according to

clearly defined rules.

"Measurement is "the act or process of assigning a number or category to an entity to describe an attribute of that entity."

Fundamental measurement is a means by which numbers can be assigned according to natural laws to represent the property, and yet which does not presuppose measurement of any other variables" than the one being measured.

5. Measurement of CK Metrics

"Measurement is the assignment of numbers to objects or events according to rule. [4] The rule of assignment can be any consistent rule. The only rule not allowed would be random assignment, for randomness amounts in effect to a nonrule."

"Measurement is the process of empirical, objective, assignment of numbers to properties of objects or events of the real world in such a way as to describe them."

"Measurement is the process by which numbers or symbols are assigned to attributes of entities in the real world in such a way as to characterize them according to clearly defined rules."

Measurement is "the act or process of assigning a number or category to an entity to describe an attribute of that entity."

IEEE Standard lays out a methodology for developing metrics for software quality attributes. The standard defines an *attribute* as "a measurable physical or abstract property of an entity." A *quality factor* is a type of attribute, "a management-oriented attribute of software that contributes to its quality." A metric is a measurement function, and a software quality metric is "a function whose inputs are software data and whose output is a single numerical value that can be interpreted as the degree to which software possesses a given attribute that affects its quality."

5.1 The CK Metrics Suite

Chidamber and Kemerer developd a suite of class oriented metrics. There are six class-based metric for OO codes.

Weighted methods per class (WMC):

It is the sum of the complexities of all methods of a class. According to this metric if a Class C, has n methods and c1, c2 ... cn be the complexity of the methods, then WMC(C)= c1 + c2 +... + cn. Mc Cabe's complexity metric is chosen for calculating the complexity values of the methods of a class. The value is normalized so that nominal complexity for a method takes on a value of 1.0. If all method complexities are considered to be unity, then WMC = n i.e. the number of methods existing in that class.

Depth of the inheritance tree (DIT):

Depth of inheritance of a class is "the maximum length from the node to the root of the tree". More is the depth of the inheritance tree greater the reusability of the class corresponding to the root of that tree as the class properties are shared by more derived classes under that class. So there too much depth dilutes the abstraction. So there is a need to set the minimum & maximum DIT value for a class as an contribution towards the reusability.

The definition of DIT is ambiguous when multiple inheritance and multiple roots are present as the alternative length of the path is not being considered in case of multiple inheritance. If we add all the ancestor classes coming in common path to the ancestor classes coming in alternative

paths then that will be the true representation of the theoretical basis of the DIT metric.

Number of Children (NOC):

According to this metric Number of children (NOC) of a class is the number of immediate sub-classes subordinated to a class in the class hierarchy. So greater is the value of NOC greater will be the reusability of the parent class. Hence there should be some minimum value of NOC for a parent class for its reusability. Theoretical basis of NOC metric relates to the notion of scope of properties. It is a measure of how many sub-classes are going to inherit the methods of the parent class. The definition of NOC metric gives the distorted view of the system as it counts only the immediate sub-classes instead of all the descendants of the class. NOC value of a class, say class i, should reflect all the subclasses that share the properties of that class.

$NOC(i) = N + \Sigma_i^{\text{All subclasses}} NOC(i)$

Where N is the total number of immediate subclasses of class i.

Coupling between object classes (CBO):

It is the number of coupled classes.

Response for a class (RFC):

According to this metric "Coupling Between Object Classes" (CBO) for a class is a count of the number of other classes to which it is coupled. Theoretical basis of CBO relates to the notion that an object is coupled to another object if one of them acts on the other, i.e. methods of one object use methods or instance variables of another. Here we are restricting the unidirectional use of methods or instance variables of another object by the object of the class whose reusability is to be measured. As Coupling between Object classes increases, reusability decreases and it becomes harder to modify and test the software system. So there is the need to set some maximum value of coupling level for its reusability. If the value of CBO for a class is beyond that maximum value then the class is said to be non-reusable. It is the number of methods that can be triggered by a message sent to an object.

Lack of cohesion in methods (LCOM):

Consider a Class C1 with *n* methods M1 , M2 ..., Mn . Let {Ij } be set of instance variables used by method Mi .There are *n* such sets {I1},{I2}... {In}. Let P = { (Ii ,Ij) | Ii ∩ Ij = ∅ } and Q = { (Ii ,Ij) | Ii ∩ Ij ≠ ∅ }. If all n sets {I1},{I2}... {In}. are ∅ then let P = ∅ [4].

Lack of Cohesion in Methods (LCOM) of a class can be defined as

LCOM = |P| - |Q|, if |P| > |Q|

LCOM = 0 otherwise

The high value of LCOM indicates that the methods in the class are not really related to each other and vice versa means less reusability otherwise low value of LCOM depicts high

internal strength of the class which results into high reusability. So there should be some maximum value of LCOM after which class becomes non-reusable.

5.2 Introduction of the Tool used

5.2.1 CKJM Tool

The program *ckjm* calculates Chidamber and Kemerer object-oriented metrics by processing the bytecode of compiled Java files. The program calculates for each class six metrics proposed by Chidamber and Kemerer. It is an open-source Java bytecode parser which uses the Apache Byte Code Engineering Library (http)/jakarta.apache.org/bcel). The tool is called Chidamber Kemerer Java Metrics (ckjm) which can be found at (http://www.spinellis.gr/sw/ckjm). To run the program you simply specify the class files (or pairs of jar/class files) on its command line or standard input. The program will produce on its standard output a line for each class containing the complete name of the class and the values of its metrics. This operation model allows the tool to be easilly extended using textual pre- and post-processors.It computes the entire Chidamber and Kemerer metric suite along with the number of public methods per class and afferent coupling (similar to the efferent CBO). This tool was used to verify that the implemented CBO representation was accurate at measuring CBO correctly.

5.2.2 Eclipse Metrics Plug-In

The CK metrics are implemented using the Eclipse (http://www.eclipse.org) Plug-in framework. This framework was chosen because of the Java language parser available that was able to parse the Third Java Language Specification (JLS3). Eclipse is an Integrated Development Environment (IDE) which allows any of the proposed metrics to be run while a developer is modifying their code.

Installing the Eclipse:

1. Install Eclipse 3.1 on computer system, then download and install latest version from:
   http://www.eclipse.org/downloads/
2. Update the version from menus:
   help->software updates
3. Follow initial plug in installation procedures at
   http://metrics.sourceforge.net/
   after successful installation, below mentioned eclipse image will appear.

Fig 5.1: Eclipse image

To start using the Metrics View, use Windows -> Show View -> Other and navigate to the Metrics View, as shown in the next image.

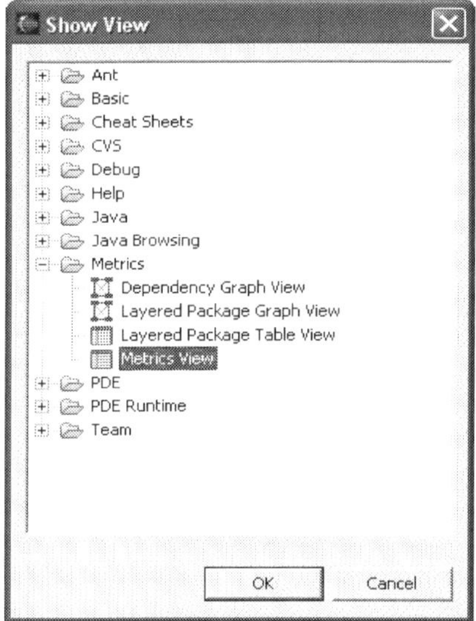

Fig 5.2: how to enable metrics view

Initially the resulting view will show a brief usage message because no metrics have been calculated yet. To start collecting metrics for a project, right click on the project and from the popup menu select "Metrics->Enable" (or alternatively, use the properties page).This will tell Eclipse to calculate metrics every time a compile happens. Now that you've enabled a project, the easiest way to calculate all its metrics is to do a full rebuild of that project.

First of all, we will import our source code that is to be calculated. In the following diagram, java source code is shown which calculates the software quality factors. Equations for calculating te factors are used in this code.

```
public int getFlexibility() {
    int a=1,b=1,c=1,d=1;
    Flexibility=(a*dit+b*noc-c*cbo+d*lcom);
    return flexibility;
}

public int getMaintainability() {
     int a=1,b=1,c=1,d=1,e=1,f=1;
     maintainability=(a*dit+b*noc+c*cbo+d*lcom+e*rfc+f*wmc);
    return maintainability;
}

public int getReliability() {

    int a=1,b=1,c=1,d=1,e=1;

   reliability=a*loc+b*wmc+c*cbo+d*lcom+e*noc;

    return reliability;
}

public int getUsability() {

    int a=1,b=1,c=1,d=1,e=1;
    Usability=(a*dit+b*noc-c*cbo-d*wmc+e*loc);
    return Usability;
}
```

Fig 5.3: java source code

Next source code read CK metrics from a text file and then generates the quality factors.

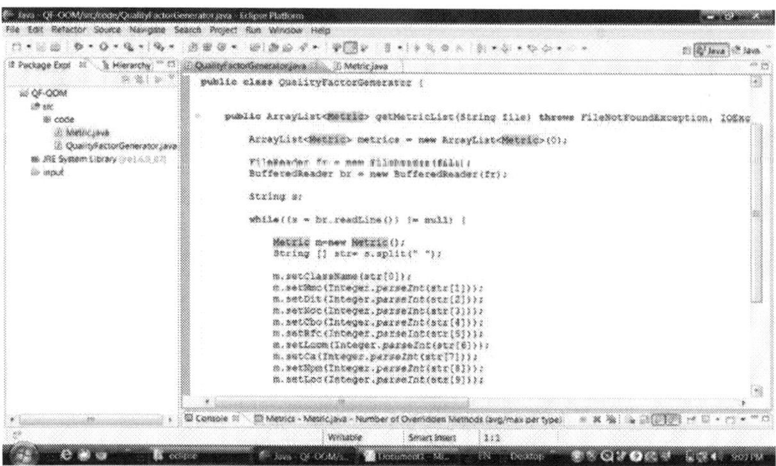

Fig 5.4:Source code for quality factors

Metrics view

To start collecting metrics for a project, right click on the project and from the popup menu select "Metrics->Enable" (or alternatively, use the properties page).This will tell Eclipse to calculate metrics every time a compile happens. Now that you've enabled a project, the easiest way to calculate all its metrics is to do a full rebuild of that project. The metrics view will indicate the progress of the metrics calculations as they are being performed in the background. The metrics view will look something like this:

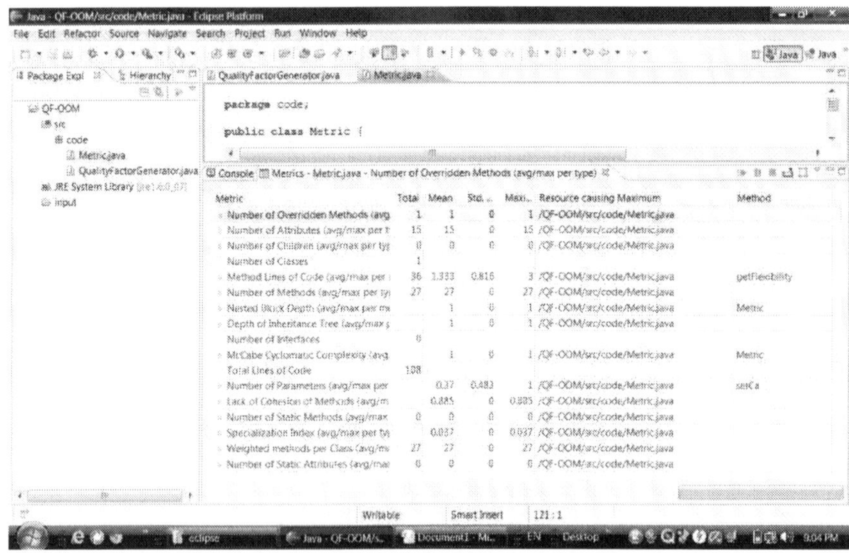

Fig5.5: Metrics view

Preferences

The metrics preferences allow the display order of the metrics to be changed and the metrics database to be cleared (to force recalculation of all metrics). In addition, the toplevel preference page serves as a category for individual metric's preference pages (net.sourceforge.metrics.ui.MetricsPreferencePage).

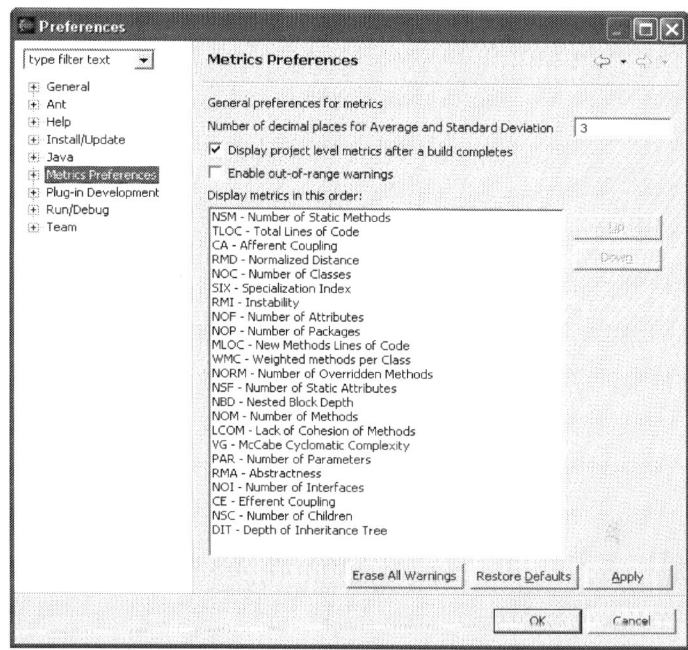

Fig 5.6: Preferences

As of version 1.0.9 of the plugin, the metrics can now trigger warnings that show up in the task view as well as the editors, indicating methods and types for which metrics safe ranges are being violated. The minimum and maximum for each metric can be set in the preferences. This feature is disabled by default, and has to be enabled on the main preference page.

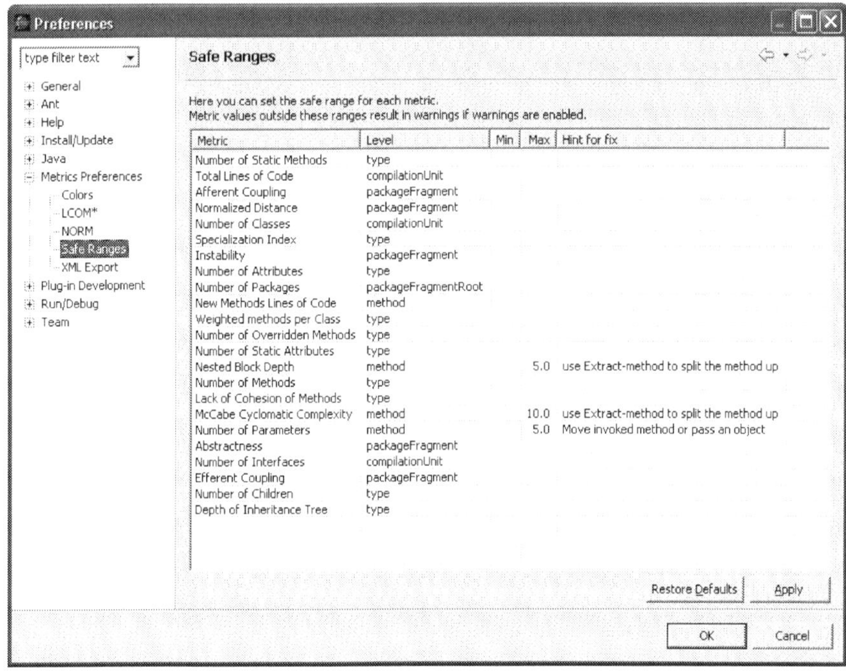

Fig 5.7: Metrics safe ranges

Exporting xml file

After getting the metrics view,these metrics are exported to an xml file. To export metrics, select the scope (project, package, etc.) so it is displayed in the view. Then use the view's toolbar or dropdown menu to select the export function. Xml file obtained will be as follows:

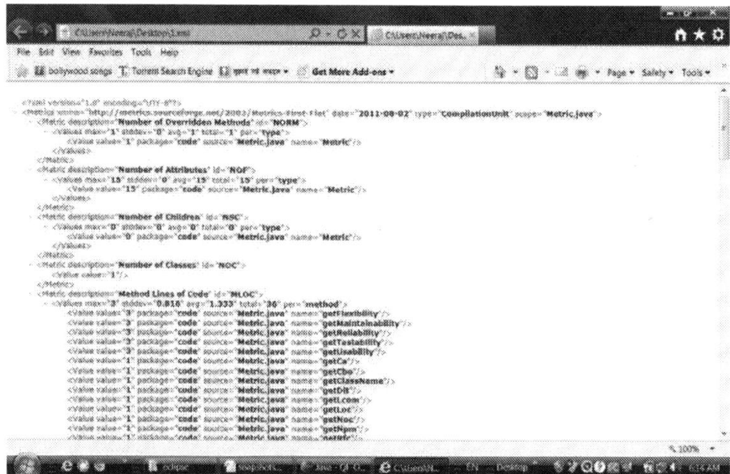

Fig 5.8: Exported Xml file

6 Measurement of software quality Factors

Software quality is comprised of many quality factors which affect it. Among these software quality factors, I will calculate software usability, maintainability, testability, reliability and software flexibility. The proposed model for measuring the quality factors is shown below:

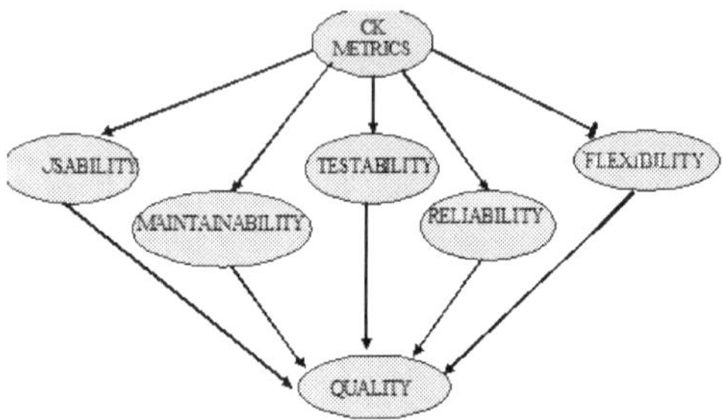

Fig 6.1: Proposed Software quality model

6.1 Measurement of Usability

Usability is defined as "The effort required to learn, operate, prepare input for and interpret output of a program". We can measure software usability with the help of CK metrics. The effect of values of CK metrics on software usability is defined in the principles below:

Principles to measure software usability are:

Deeper a particular class is in the hierarchy, the greater the potential for use of inherited methods. It states that usability increases with increase in DIT of a class. So DIT has positive impact on usability of a class.

A moderate value for NOC indicates scope for easy use [35]. Up to particular threshold value NOC has positive impact on usability of a class.

Excessive coupling indicates weakness of class encapsulation. It indicates that coupling has negative impact on usability of a class.

Larger no of weighted methods, larger will be the usability.

Based upon above principles, equation for reusability is derived as:

Usability of a class = a_1*(DIT) + b_1*(NOC) – c_1*(CBO)+d_1*(WMC)+e_1*(LOC)

= 0 when < 1

where a_1, b_1, c_1 are regression constants; initially we consider $a_1 = b_1 = c_1 = 1$ ---- (6.1)

Usability of OO program = sum(usability(class)$_i$)

where i = 1 to n, n is number of classes ---- (6.2)

6.2. Measurement of Maintainability

Maintainability is defined as "the effort required to locate and fix an error in a program".

Thus maintainability is measured in the form of maintainability effort with the help of CK metrics. The effect of values of CK metrics on maintainability effort is defined in the principles below:

Principles for measuring Maintainability Effort are:

The larger the DIT metric, the harder it is to maintain the class [22].

The more direct children a class has, the more classes it may potentially effect because of inheritance and hence be harder to maintain [22].

Higher the RFC, the harder to maintain because of it being more difficult to trace with a lot of method calls and responses [22].

If LCOM is high it may be that the class is badly designed and partitioned and hence hard to maintain [22].

The more methods in a class the more complex the class is, and hence harder to maintain [22].

The more CBO a class has the more complex the coupling of that class with other classes, hence harder to maintain [22].

Based upon above principles equation for Maintainability Effort is derived as follows:

Maintainability effort of a class = a_2*(DIT) + b_2*(NOC) + c_2*(CBO) +d_2*(LCOM) + e_2*(RFC) + f_2*(WMC)

where a_2, b_2, c_2, d_2, e_2, f_2 are regression constants;

initially, we will consider $a_2 = b_2 = c_2 = d_2 = e_2 = f_2 = 1$ ----- (6.3)

Maintainability effort of OO program = sum (maintainability _effort(class)$_i$)

where i = 1 to n, n is number of classes ----- (6.4)

3.1.3. Measurement of Testability

Testability is defined as "the effort required to test a program to ensure that it performs its intended function". Thus testability is also measured in form of testability effort. The effect of values of CK metrics on testability is defined in the principles below:

Principles for measuring Testability are:

LOC, the larger the size of a class, more effort is required to test a class [23].

WMC, more the methods in a class, more difficult it is to test the class [23].

CBO, more testing effort is required where there is more coupling [23]

Based upon these principles, equations for measuring testability are following:

Testability of a class = a_3*(LOC) + b_3*(WMC) + c_3*(CBO)

where a_3, b_3, c_3 are regression constants

$a_3 = b_3 = c_3 = 1$ ----- (6.5)

Testability of OO program = sum(testability(class)$_i$)

where i = 1 to n, n is number of classes ------ (6.6)

3.1.4. Measurement of Reliability

Reliability is defined as "The extent to which a program can be expected to perform its intended function with required precision". Reliability is predicted from the fault proneness of the class. More the class is fault prone, lesser reliable it is. The effect of values of CK metrics on fault proneness is defined in the principles below:

The principles for measuring fault proneness are following:

LOC, larger classes are more prone to faults [21].

WMC, greater the number of methods in class, greater are the chances of faults in them.

LCOM, less cohesive classes are having greater chances of faults in them [21].

NOC, more children a class has, more fault prone it is [21].

CBO, a class with high CBO tends to be more fault prone [21].

Classes with having large fault proneness are having less reliability.

Based upon above principles, the equations for measuring fault proneness are following:

Fault Proneness of a class = a_4*(LOC) + b_4*(WMC) + c_4*(CBO) + d_4*(LCOM) +e_4*(NOC)

where a_4, b_4, c_4, d_4 and e_4 are empirical constants

$a_4 = b_4 = c_4 = d_4 = e_4 = 1$ ---- (6.7)

Fault Proneness of OO program = sum (fault_proneness(class)$_i$)

where i = 1 to n , n is number of classes ---- (6.8)

Measurement of Flexibility

The ability of software to change easily in response to different user and system requirements.

The ease with which a system or component can be modified for use in applications or environments other than those for which it was specifically designed.

Flexibility of a class = a_5*(DIT) + b_5*(NOC) – c_5*(CBO) + d_5*(LCOM)

where a_5, b_5, c_5, d_5 are regression coefficients.

$a_5 = b_5 = c_5 = d_5 = 1$ ---- (6.9)

Flexibility of OO program = sum (flexibility $(class)_i$)

where i = 1 to n , n is number of classes ---- (6.10)

Measurement using Eclipse platefom

Eclipse metric lug in is applicable to java applications.java source code is required to calculate Factors.

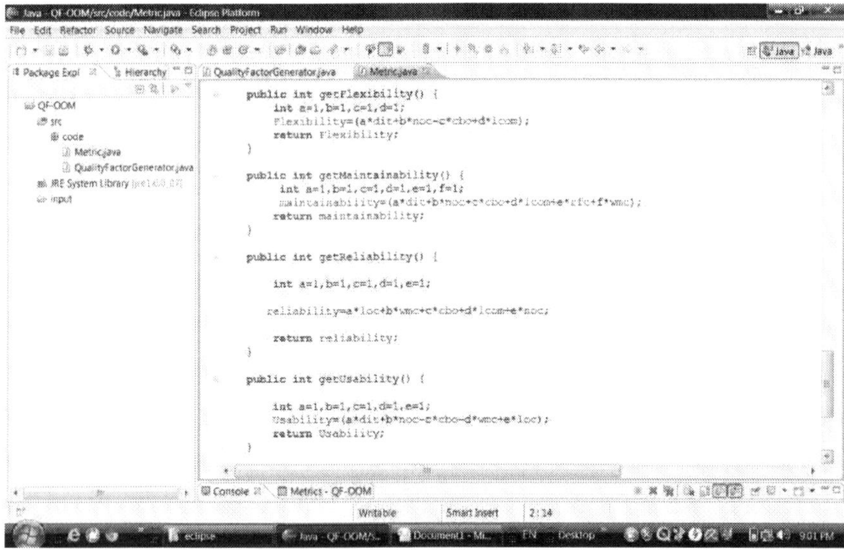

Fig 6.2: source code

To calculate quality factors ,I have java code QualityFactorGenerator which read ck metrics from a text file.ck metric are given as input to the program.

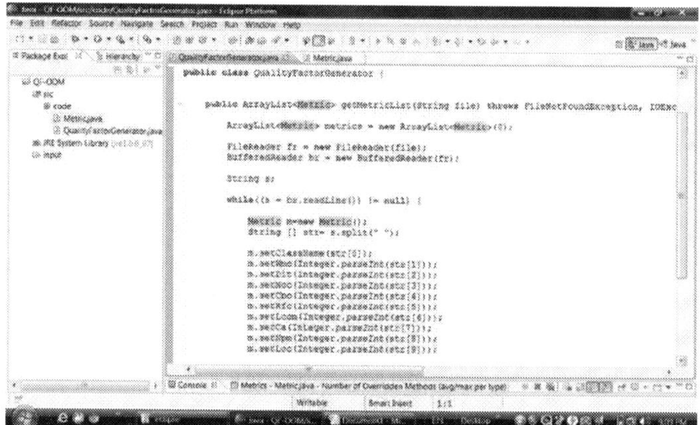

Fig 6.3: QualityfactorGenerator code

After getting exported xml file,a text file is prepared so that ck metrics can be easily read from the program. This text file is the combination of metrics obtained by ckjm and eclipse metric tools.

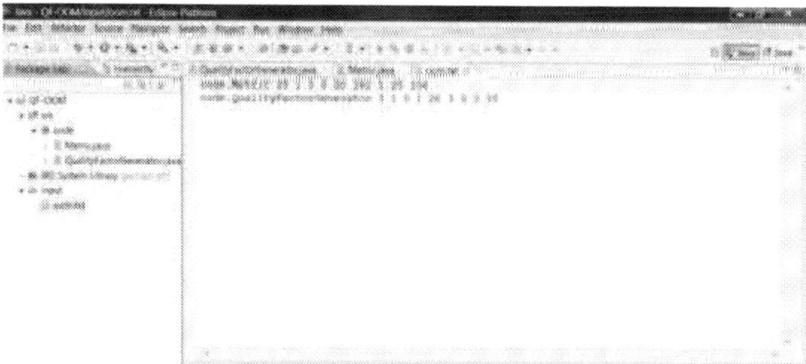

Fig 6.4: Metric Text file

After running the program,quality factors are generated.we can see the quality factors generated from the console view.

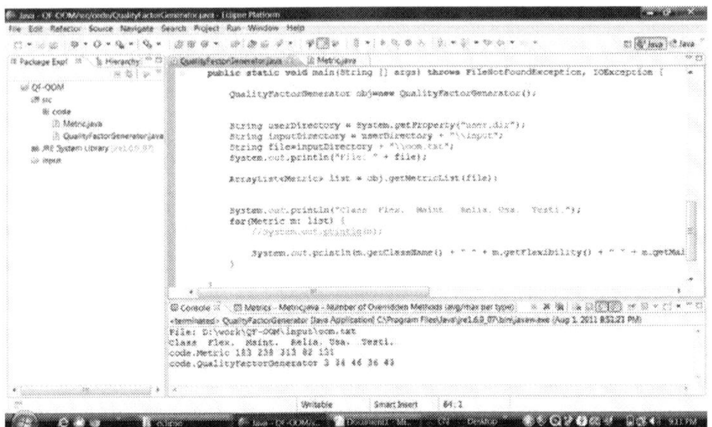

Fig 6.5: Quality factors

7. CONCLUSIONS AND FUTURE SCOPE

In this dissertation work, we have proposed software quality model. Software Quality involves characteristics of indirect measurement and cannot be measured directly. We have taken McCall's Model as our basic model and measured its different quality attributes with CK metrics. Linear equations are derived from CK metrics to measure these quality attributes. Ckjm and eclipse metrics tool are used to calculate ck metrics. It has been analyzed that usability is good for those OO examples that are having high inheritance and low coupling. Maintainability is low for examples that are having low coupling, high cohesion and low inheritance. Testability is low for examples that are having small size and low coupling. Examples that are having small size, low coupling and high cohesion are less fault prone and hence more reliable. Examples that are having high inheritance, low coupling and high cohesion are having high flexibility. Software quality is high for examples that are small in size, having good inheritance, low coupling and high cohesion.

Hence it is proved that to develop high quality software size should be kept small, OO design should be modularized to increase inheritance, coupling among different classes should be low and the design should be highly cohesive. This research work is helpful for developers for building high quality software.

In future more quality attributes will be measured with the help of CK metrics. This can be done by adding more quality attributes in proposed Quality Model and predicting relationships between quality attributes.

REFERENCES

1. Chidamber, S. R. and Kemerer, C. F., "Towards a metrics suite for object oriented design," in Proc. 6th ACM Conf. Object Oriented Programming. Syst., Lung. and Applicat. (OOPSLA), Phoenix, AZ, 1991, pp. 197-21

2. Chidamber, S. R. and Kemerer, C. F., "A Metric Suite for Object-Oriented Design," IEEE Transactions on Software Engineering, 20(6):476-493, 1994.

3. Rosenberg, L., "Applying and Interpreting Object Oriented Metrics", Software Assurance Technology Center, NASA Goddard Space Flight Center, Greenbelt, Maryland 20771

4. McCabe, T. J., "A Complexity Measure", IEEE Transactions on Software Engineering, SE -2(4), pages 308-320, December 1976.

5. McCall, J. A., Richards, P. K., and Walters, G. F., "Factors in Software Quality", Nat'l Tech. Information Service, no. Vol. 1, 2 and 3, 1977.

6. Booch, G., Object Oriented Design with Applications. Redwood City, CA: Benjamin/ Cummings, 1991.

7. P. Coad and E. Yourdon, Object-Oriented Design. Englewood Cliffs, NJ: Prentice-Hall, 1991.

8. E. Weyuker, "Evaluating software complexity measures," IEEE Transactions on Software Engineering, vol. 14, pp. 1357-1365, 1988

9. C. F. Kemerer, "Reliability of function points measurement: A field experiment," Commum. ACM, vol. 36, pp. 85-97, 1993.

10. Churcher, N. L., and Shepperd, M. J., " Comments on a Metric suite for Object Oriented Design" IEEE Transactions on Software Engineering, vol. 21, pp. 263-265, 1995.

11. Hitz, M., and Montazeri, B., "C&K metrics suite: a measurement theory perspective" IEEE Transactions on Software Engineering, vol. 22, pp. 267-271, 1996.

12. Graham, I. M., "Making progress in metrics", Object Magazine, pp. 68-73, 1996.

13. Henderson-Sellers, B., "Object-Oriented Metrics: Measures of Complexity", Prentice- Hall Object Oriented Series, 1996.

14. R. Harrison, S.J. Counsell, R. V. Nithi, "An Investigation into the Applicability and Validity of Object Oriented Design Metrics", Empirical Software Engineering, vol. 3, pp. 255-273, 1998.

15. Rosenberg, Linda H. and Hyatt, Lawrence E. " Software Quality metrics for Object Oriented Environment",http://satc.gsfc.nasa.gov/support/CROSS_APR97/oocross.PDF

16. Rosenberg, L., and Hyatt, L., "Software Quality Metrics for Object-Oriented System Environments", Software Assurance Technology Center, Technical Report SATC-TR-95-1001, NASA Goddard Space Flight Center, Greenbelt, Maryland 20771

17. N.E. Fenton, "Software Metrics: A Rigorous Approach", New York, Chapman & Hall, 1991

18. Pressman, Roger S., Software Engineering, A Practitioner's Approach, McGraw-Hill Publishing, 19xx.

19. Jalote, P., "An Integrated Approach to Software Engineering". Springer-Verlag, 1991.

20. M. Shooman, Software Engineering. McGraw-Hill, 1983.

21. Ping Yu, Tarja Syst¨a and Hausi M¨uller, "Predicting Fault Proneness using OO Metrics: An Industrial Case Study", Proceedings of the Sixth European Conference on Software Maintenance and Reengineering (CSMR.02), 1534-5351/02

22. Wei Li and Sallie Henry, "Object Oriented Metrics that Predict Maintainability", Journal on Systems Software vol 23, pp. 111-122, 1993.

23. Magiel Bruntink, Arie van Deursen, "Predicting Class Testability using Object-Oriented Metrics" Proceedings of the Fourth IEEE International Workshop on Source Code Analysis and Manipulation (SCAM'04), pp 1-10, 2004

24. Prem Devanbu, Sakke Karstu, WalcClio Melo and William Thomas, "Analytical and Empirical Evaluation of Software Reuse Metrics". Proceedings of ICSE-18, pp 189-199, 1996.

25. J. R. Mckee, "Maintenance as a Function of Design". Proceedings AFIPS, National Computer Conference, Las Vegas, pp 187-93.

26. Ian Sommerville, "Software Engineering", 5th Ed., Addison Wesley, 1996.

27. J. Voas, "PIE: A dynamic failure-based technique." IEEE transactions on Software Engineering. 18(8): 717-727, August 1992.

28. Krishan K. Aggarwal, Yogesh Singh, Jitender Kumar Chhabra, "An Integrated Measure of Software Maintainability." Proceedings of Annual Reliability and Maintainability Symposium. Pg 235-241, 2002

29. Jaydev Gyani and N. Sambasiva Rao, "Object Oriented Reuse Metrics- A study on Inheritance."

30. Musa, J.D., A. Iannino and K. Okumoto, Software Reliability: Measurement, Prediction, Application, Professional Edition: Software Engineering Series, McGraw–Hill, New York, NY., 1990.

31. Triantafyllos, G., S. Vassiliadis and W. Kobrosly, "On the Prediction of Computer Implementation Faults Via Static Error Prediction Models," Journal of Systems and Software, Vol. 28, No. 2, February 1995, pp. 129-142.

32. Waterman, R.E and L.E. Hyatt, "Testing - When Do I Stop?" (Invited) International Testing and Evaluation Conference, Washington, DC, October 1994.

33. Dr. Linda Rosenberg, Ted Hammer, Jack Shaw, "Software Reliability and Metrics," satc.gsfc.nasa.gov/support/ISSRE_NOV98/software_metrics_and_reliability.html

34. ISO 9126 Software Quality Characteristics, www.sqa.net/iso9126.html

35. Liang,V., and Colemon, C., “Principal Components of Orthogonal Object Oriented Metrics”, Software Assurance Technology Center, White Paper SATC-323-08-14, NASA Goddard Space Flight Center, Greenbelt, Maryland 20771.

Made in the USA
Columbia, SC
27 November 2024